The Entertainment Ministry

PRESENTS

GILLIGAN'S ISLAND & THE SEVEN DEADLY SINS Bible Study

study guide

WRITER: ***Stephen Skelton***

CREATIVE: ***Jim Howell, Judy Northcutt Gaertner***

Gilligan's Island and the Seven Deadly Sins
PUBLISHED BY ***The Entertainment Ministry, LLC***

Printed in the United States of America

ISBN 978-0-9791259-5-9

OTHER STUDIES AVAILABLE

The Mayberry Bible Study

The Beverly Hillbillies Bible Study

The Lucy Show Bible Study

The Van Dyke Show Bible Study

The Bonanza Bible Study

The Super Man Bible Study

CHARLES DICKENS' ***A Christmas Carol Bible Study***

ABOUT THE AUTHOR

Stephen Skelton, founder of The Entertainment Ministry, serves as host for *Gilligan's Island & The Seven Deadly Sins*. Previously, he has served as a writer-producer with Dick Clark Productions and later as host and writer of Bible studies based on *Mayberry*, *Beverly Hillbillies, Lucy Show, Van Dyke Show*, *Bonanza, Super Man* and *Charles Dickens' A Christmas Carol.* As a Christian in the entertainment industry, Stephen seeks to identify God's purposes in popular entertainment. Stephen lives in Nashville, Tennessee with his wife and children.

ABOUT THE ENTERTAINMENT MINISTRY

At The Entertainment Ministry, we believe many stories that transcend social, racial and cultural barriers today do so because they contain spiritual truth for which all people have a God-given hunger. Accordingly, the ministry promotes a grassroots approach to using popular entertainment to engage a Christian worldview. To that end, we hope these Bible studies not only provide a time of good fellowship, but also continue to equip the church with ways to reach the world beyond.

THE STORY

This section, **"Rescue from Gilligan's Island,"** shows the seven deadly sins of our seven stranded Castaways as they finally get the chance to go home! But before they escape the island, predictably, Gilligan gets lazy, the Skipper becomes angry, the Professor grows prideful, Ginger incites lust, Mary Ann envies Ginger, Mr. Howell gets greedy and Lovey Howell gets gluttonous. You'll be amazed at how our seven stranded Castaways really do comically commit the seven deadly sins!

THE MORAL OF THE STORY

*This lesson, **"Seven Castaways, Seven Deadly Sins,"** highlights the Biblical principles of the Seven Deadly Sins. The notes focus on the seven sins that were considered deadly because they can kill the life of grace that the Lord wants us to live. The study then examines sloth, anger, pride, greed, gluttony, lust and envy. In closing, this lesson also points out the seven holy virtues that stand against the seven deadly sins: diligence, patience, humility, chastity, generosity, restraint and contentment.*

GILLIGAN'S ISLAND & THE SEVEN DEADLY SINS
Bible Study

lesson 1

SECTION TITLE: **"Rescue from Gilligan's Island"**

LESSON TITLE: **"Seven Castaways, Seven Deadly Sins"**

BIBLICAL PRINCIPLES: **Sloth, Anger, Pride, Greed, Gluttony, Lust and Envy**

7 DEADLY SINS...

MARK 7:21-23
"For from within, out of men's hearts, come evil thoughts, sexual immorality, theft, murder, adultery, greed, malice, deceit, lewdness, envy, slander, arrogance and folly. All these evils come from inside and make a man 'unclean.'"

Proverbs 20:4
A sluggard does not plow in season; so at harvest time he looks but finds nothing.

"The Castaways were symbolic of the Seven Deadly Sins."
Sherwood Schwartz, creator of *Gilligan's Island*

Parable / *A Three Hour Tour...*

Early Christian teachers considered seven sins deadly. (And before we get too relieved their list only included seven, be warned—they're the big ones.) **While the Bible does not list the seven sins by themselves, the teaching was derived from passages like the one cited, in which 1) greed is represented by "greed;" 2) envy is represented by "envy;" 3) lust is represented by "sexual immorality," "adultery" and "lewdness;" 4) anger is represented by "murder" and "malice;" 5) pride is represented by "arrogance;" 6) gluttony (hoarding resources at the expense of others) is represented by "theft;" and 7) sloth (laziness) is represented by "folly"(Mk 7:21-23).** These sins were called deadly because they can damage our capacity to love, thereby causing serious injury to our relationships to God and men, and thus killing the life of grace that the Lord wants us to live.

Gilligan

SLOTH...

Lazy people don't think they're lazy—they don't put that much work into it. Unfortunately, sloth (or laziness) is a condition that affects us not only physically and mentally, but spiritually. Without a purpose, an aimless life is vulnerable to many sinful distractions. ***In contrast, God wants to provide a direction for our lives, so that we can be strong, responsible and prepared (Pr 20:4).*** *Consider the ways in which Gilligan acted slothfully.*

Was Gilligan diligent or directionless? Were his actions with the barometer disk and the rescue fire intentional or accidental? How so?

The Skipper

ANGER...

Angry people simply care too much—about themselves. Often when we get angry, we are more focused on ourselves than what God wants us to do about the needs of those around us. ***This is how anger trades love for fury, like Jonah who cared more about a withered vine than a city full of people (Jnh 4:4).*** *Tellingly, when we get angry like this, we actually anger God, who is angered by only one thing: our sin. Think about why the Skipper got angry.*

Why did the Skipper get angry at Gilligan?
For whose sake did the Skipper get angry?

Jonah 4:4
But the LORD replied [to Jonah], "Have you any right to be angry?"

The Professor

PRIDE...

Too much pride is nothing to be proud of. The danger of this sin is that it stops us from acknowledging the grace of God by convincing us that we are sufficient on our own. ***This false sense of importance is why pride ultimately brings men low—all of the things we value are temporary: money, power, prestige, appearances—while those that depend on the Lord gain eternal honor in his eyes (Pr 29:23).*** *Recall how the Professor revealed his pride.*

How was the Professor prideful?
Why did he think only he could come up with a rescue plan?

Proverbs 29:23
A man's pride brings him low, but a man of lowly spirit gains honor.

Schwartz described *Gilligan's Island* as a comedy on top and allegory underneath.

Ephesians 5:5
For of this you can be sure: No immoral, impure or greedy person—such a man is an idolater—has any inheritance in the kingdom of Christ and of God.

Thurston Howell III

GREED...

The feeling of greed can never be satisfied by an act of greed. ***This is because, more than any one potential possession, greed idolizes greed, making the greedy person an idolater (Eph 5:5).*** *The subtle deceit of greed is that it causes us to concentrate on the material world at the expense of keeping a focus on the spiritual realm. A person afflicted by such blindness will never see the kingdom of God. Remember how Mr. Howell encouraged greed.*

How did Mr. Howell show his focus on greed?
Why did he try to bribe Gilligan?

Proverbs 28:7
He who keeps the law is a discerning son, but a companion of gluttons disgraces his father.

Lovey Howell

GLUTTONY...

Gluttons desire more than they require. It is a selfishness beyond satiation for anything, whether food or riches or even social standing. Gluttony can also corrupt businesses and governments, causing them to mistreat many to benefit a few. ***Whether on a personal or national level, this type of injustice is disgraceful to God, who will not forget the sinner's selfishness (Pr 28:7).*** *To tweak a popular phrase: in the end, all gluttons are gluttons for punishment. Consider how Lovey Howell indulged in gluttony.*

How did Mrs. Howell engage in gluttony?
Why would she want to count her servants at home?

"With broad comedy, it's easier to get messages across."
Sherwood Schwartz

Ginger

LUST...

Those in lust may think it is love gone cheap—the truth is, lust never makes it that far. While love is something more than physical pleasures, lust makes even those physical pleasures something less than they are. ***Our sexual desires should be placed under God's guidance and our sexual experience should take place within marriage—which will keep us from hurting God and others, as well as ourselves (1 Th 4:3-5).*** *Think about how Ginger used lust.*

Why did Ginger try to entice Gilligan with lust?
How did she try to tempt him to tell his secret?

1 Thessalonians 4:3-5
It is God's will that you should be sanctified: that you should avoid sexual immorality; 4) that each of you should learn to control his own body in a way that is holy and honorable, 5) not in passionate lust like the heathen, who do not know God;

Mary Ann

ENVY...

Envy is evil—and evil is often what envious people envy. When wicked men prosper through wicked means, it is tempting to want what they've got, regardless of how they got it. ***But we should remember that those men have no future hope—while everything they have that we envy will fade, to add injury to insult, God will still punish them for the sins they committed to get it (Pr 24:19-20).*** *Recall how Mary Ann dealt with envy.*

Why did Mary Ann try to inspire envy in Gilligan?
Why did she tease him with her pies?

Proverbs 24:19-20
Do not fret because of evil men or be envious of the wicked, 20) for the evil man has no future hope, and the lamp of the wicked will be snuffed out.

SPECIAL NOTE **SEVEN HOLY VIRTUES**

Briefly, in opposition to the seven deadly sins, early Christian teachers also compiled a list of seven holy virtues. Living out these virtues was meant to help men counteract the temptation toward the seven sins. Those seven virtues are as follow: 1) **diligence**—against sloth, 2) **patience**—against anger, 3) **chastity**—against lust, 4) **humility**—against pride, 5) **generosity**—against greed, 6) **restraint**—against gluttony and 7) **contentment**—against envy. The next sections of our study will further illustrate this dynamic between the seven deadly sins and the seven holy virtues.

Rescue from Gilligan's Island remains one of the highest rated film specials in television history.

THE STORY

This section, **"Gilligan & the Skipper,"** presents our two crewmen not only at their wacky worst—lazy & angry—but also their unexpected best—diligent & patient! At work on their new boat, Gilligan varnishes a deckchair—only to have the Skipper get his seat stuck in that seat! Then the dysfunctional duo learns the insurance company has rejected their claim on the first *Minnow*, demanding that all the Castaways confirm the report of the wreck! So the "one who snoozes" and the "one who loses it" set off to reunite with their friends.

THE MORAL OF THE STORY

*This lesson, **"You Snooze. You Lose It.,"** highlights the Biblical principles of Sloth and Anger. The study examines how sloth is sinful because it refuses to engage God, and anger is sinful because it allows Satan a chance to drive us apart. The lesson also explains that anger presents a corruption of love, while sloth shows an apathetic absence of any love at all. The point of this study is that the instruction found in the Bible on both sloth and anger is self-preserving: the slothful must be diligent; the angry must be patient.*

GILLIGAN'S ISLAND & THE SEVEN DEADLY SINS

Bible Study

lesson 2

SECTION TITLE: **"Gilligan & the Skipper"**

LESSON TITLE: **"You Snooze. You Lose It."**

BIBLICAL PRINCIPLES: **Sloth & Anger**

SLOTH...

PROVERBS 6:9
How long will you lie there, you sluggard? When will you get up from your sleep?

ANGER...

EPHESIANS 4:26-27
"In your anger do not sin": Do not let the sun go down while you are still angry, and do not give the devil a foothold.

Proverbs 14:29
A patient man has great understanding, but a quick-tempered man displays folly.

The hardest role to cast was the Skipper because, according to the producer, the role required a delicate balance between Attila the Hun and Santa Claus—which actor Alan Hale had.

Parable / *A Three Hour Tour...*

Sloth and anger—one person cares too little about others, and the other cares too much about himself. Of sloth (laziness), the Bible does not say that we should never rest—God gave us a weekly day of rest on the Sabbath. Of anger, the Bible does not say that we should never get angry—Christ got angry at hypocritical religious leaders. The sin arises in how we apply each: when we rest too much or get angry for the wrong reasons. **Sloth—whether physical, mental or spiritual—is sinful because of its refusal to engage God, which not only hampers religious diligence but also causes a general dissatisfaction with life (Pr 6:9). Similarly, anger is sinful when it is ignited so rashly and expressed so badly that it allows Satan a chance to drive us apart (Eph 4:26-27).**

By varnishing the seat, was Gilligan being lazy or diligent? Did he want to just get through or to be thorough?

Patience opposes anger—it is the holy virtue that stands against the deadly vice. Whereas anger separates us, we are drawn to a man of patience. ***This is because patience demonstrates a depth of understanding—of self, of others, of life. By contrast, anger usually demonstrates a quick judgment based on a personal offense (Pr 14:29).*** *Consider how the Skipper tried to stymie anger with patience.*

Despite his outbursts, how did the Skipper show patience? How did he throttle back his anger?

Anger can be the right reaction. ***Jesus gave us an example: he became angry unselfishly when he saw uncaring attitudes; he dealt with his feelings immediately by addressing the issue; and he acted constructively instead of destructively (Mk 3:4-5).*** *Likewise, in dealing with anger, we should pray for God to help us control our tempers, express our feelings well and channel our actions. Think about how the Skipper responded to the letter from the insurance company.*

Was the Skipper right to get angry at the insurance company?
How was truth being challenged?

Reflection / *Your Inner Gilligan...*

Sloth and anger are self-destructive. **Without instruction, a lazy man will waste the time he should be working—until a time of need, when he will find he has earned nothing with which he can support himself (Pr 19:15-16). Without instruction, an angry man will be slow to listen, quick to speak and quick to become angry—and in doing so, he will endanger his life, likely on earth and certainly in heaven (Jas 1:19-20).** Fortunately, the instruction found in the Bible on both sloth and anger is self-preserving: the slothful must be diligent; the angry must be patient. Thus, in a very practical way, obeying God is self-preserving while disobeying his teaching is self-defeating.

Like Gilligan, have you been lazy—mentally, physically or spiritually?
Give an example.

Mark 3:4-5
Then Jesus asked them, "Which is lawful on the Sabbath: to do good or to do evil, to save life or to kill?" But they remained silent. 5) He looked around at them in anger...

SLOTH...

PROVERBS 19:15-16
Laziness brings on deep sleep, and the shiftless man goes hungry. He who obeys instructions guards his life, but he who is contemptuous of his ways will die.

ANGER...

JAMES 1:19-20
My dear brothers, take note of this: Everyone should be quick to listen, slow to speak and slow to become angry, for man's anger does not bring about the righteous life that God desires.

Proverbs 19:11
A man's wisdom gives him patience; it is to his glory to overlook an offense.

At first, the Skipper seemed impatient to get angry. Indeed, the practice of patience is in part a matter of overlooking offenses. ***Anger at personal offenses reveals a lack of faith that God is in control of your life. Conversely, patience can indicate your faith in the fact that the Lord will use you for his purpose. This is how a man's wisdom gives him patience (Pr 19:11).*** *To overlook an offense, look over it to God.*

Like the Skipper at first, have you showed anger when you should have showed patience? Give an example.

Romans 2:7-8
To those who by persistence in doing good seek glory, honor and immortality, he will give eternal life. 8) But for those who are self-seeking and who reject the truth and follow evil, there will be wrath and anger.

In his anger, the Skipper wasn't always wrong. We should become angry when sinful actions occur, such as a miscarriage of justice or a distortion of the truth. The breaking of these principles goes far beyond personal offenses. ***Ideals like justice and truth are principles of God, which must not be challenged or violated. Remember, God will reward those that do good, but those that follow evil will incur his wrath (Ro 2:7-8).*** *If it angers God, it should anger us also.*

Like the Skipper, have you gotten angry for the right reasons? Give an example.

"If I had submitted to the pressures of various executives, every single character in *Gilligan's Island,* without exception, would have been changed." Sherwood Schwartz

Action / ***Living On the Island...***

For two sins that show a lack of judgment in men, both sloth and anger draw a hard judgment from God. This is because both sloth and anger break the Lord's command to love. While anger, like many of the other seven deadly sins, presents a selfish corruption of love, sloth is the only sin to show an apathetic absence of love. **A lazy man becomes poor in not only materials but spirit (Pr 10:4-5). And an angry man is judged in not only deed but thought (Mt 5:21-22).** However, both sins can be opposed by their counter virtues. If you are lazy, you should be diligent, seeing life as a gift from God and using it in loving service to him. If you are angry, you should be patient, taking a second look at whether you are reacting to evil which hurts all men or rather a petty insult that offends only you.

Why should you not be lazy?

How can you stop being angry?

How can sloth and anger destroy you?

SLOTH...

PROVERBS 10:4-5
Lazy hands make a man poor, but diligent hands bring wealth. He who gathers crops in summer is a wise son, but he who sleeps during harvest is a disgraceful son.

ANGER...

MATTHEW 5:21-22
"You have heard that it was said to the people long ago, 'Do not murder, and anyone who murders will be subject to judgment.' But I tell you that anyone who is angry with his brother, will be subject to judgment...."

Bad Idea #1:
The studio executives said the Skipper should never blow-up at Gilligan—rather, he had to be nice all the time.

THE STORY

This section, **"Ginger,"** spotlights the chastity of the movie star as she finds she doesn't want to tempt Hollywood with a comeback—because Hollywood wants to tempt the audience with too much lust! When Ginger objects to a filthy script, the movie producer argues that he is just keeping up with the times. But after Gilligan accidentally points out that wholesome movies have been big hits, the producer realizes it is okay for Ginger to say: I Don't Lust You Anymore.

THE MORAL OF THE STORY

*This lesson, **"I Don't Lust You Anymore,"** highlights the Biblical principle of Lust. The notes look at how our lust is sinful because it lessens the love that is due to God by distracting us with a cheap substitute in the flesh. This study also explains how becoming chaste involves two actions—turning from sexual sin and turning toward God. The core message here is that, once saved, we must consider ourselves dead to lust—because we are alive in Christ.*

GILLIGAN'S ISLAND & THE SEVEN DEADLY SINS
Bible Study

lesson 3

SECTION TITLE: **"Ginger"**

LESSON TITLE: **"I Don't Lust You Anymore"**

BIBLICAL PRINCIPLE: **Lust**

LUST...

PROVERBS 6:25-26
Do not lust in your heart after her beauty or let her captivate you with her eyes, for the prostitute reduces you to a loaf of bread, and the adulteress preys upon your very life.

2 Corinthians 7:1
Since we have these [God's] promises, dear friends, let us purify ourselves from everything that contaminates body and spirit, perfecting holiness out of reverence for God.

The role of Ginger, which was originally written as a slick Hollywood actress with a sarcastic wit, was later changed to be more like Marilyn-Monroe-meets-Lucille-Ball.

Parable / *A Three Hour Tour...*

Sometimes it seems our society praises lust—and thinks love is a four-letter word. Even when we're kind to love, we confuse it with lust, usually by paying lust the too-kind compliment of calling it love. However, in truth, lust and love are two very different things. Love encompasses ideals such as trust, devotion, appreciation and sacrifice. Lust is only sexual arousal. Thus, lust dehumanizes us, while love affirms our humanity. **Lust is sinful because it lessens the love that is due to God by distracting us with a cheap substitute in the flesh (Pr 6:25-26).**

Who showed lust—Ginger or the producer?
Who showed chastity? For each, how so?

Lust is a vice of indulgence. By contrast, chastity is a virtue of abstinence. While abstinence takes strength, sinful indulgence is a sign of weakness. Interestingly, unlike abstinence of sexual immorality, too much lustful indulgence usually makes a person sick, whether physically, spiritually or both. ***In this way, chastity keeps healthy the body and soul that lust would spoil (2 Cor 7:1)****. Consider what caused Ginger to turn away from lust.*

Why did Ginger object to the lustful script?
What caused her to become chaste?

Lust loves the world—and the world loves lust. Because people long to love and be loved, if we do not love God, we will love the world. ***Furthermore, whereas godliness comes from the pursuit of righteousness, worldliness arises from sinful cravings, such as lust (1 Jn 2:15-16).*** *Thus, worldliness drags us into a downward spiral—the more we indulge the world, the more the world indulges us. Finally, our highest standards match the world's lowest. Think about the producer.*

Why didn't the producer object to the lustful script?
How did he justify its contents?

1 John 2:15-16
Do not love the world or anything in the world. If anyone loves the world, the love of the Father is not in him. 16) For everything in the world—the cravings of sinful man, the lust of his eyes...comes not from the Father but from the world.

Reflection / *Your Inner Gilligan...*

Lust usually begins with a look (Job 31:1). With this simple act, you can contaminate your entire being. From the eyes, lust invades the mind, then infects the heart, then defiles the body. Equally as guilty, some invite you to lust as a means to get their way, flirting in order to gain favor. They may argue that this manipulation is all right as long as no one gets hurt—when in fact, someone is always hurt by lust. The seeming freedom to do what you want with your body is actually slavery to the desires of your body. It is better for both the looker and the one being looked at to behave chastely. By not looking lustfully or inviting lustful looks, you will be innocent of both inward and outward sins.

Like Ginger, have you used flirtation as a means to get your way?
Give an example.

LUST...

JOB 31:1
"I made a covenant with my eyes not to look lustfully at a girl."

Bad Idea #2:
The studio executives said Ginger should be a housewife instead of a movie star.

1 Corinthians 6:18-20
Flee from sexual immorality. All other sins a man commits are outside his body, but he who sins sexually sins against his own body. 19) ...You are not your own; 20) you were bought at a price. Therefore honor God with your body.

Ginger left lust. Too often, people go in search of things to incite lust. However, it is a wise man who physically removes himself from temptation. After all, your body is not your own. ***Like a rented house, you live in a property that is owned by someone else, "bought at a price" by the death of Christ for your salvation. And this landlord has rules about how his house is to be treated: what you should and should not do while you are living in his place (1 Cor 6:18-20).***

Like Ginger, have you fled from lustfulness?
Give an example.

2 Timothy 2:22
Flee the evil desires of youth, and pursue righteousness, faith, love and peace, along with those who call on the Lord out of a pure heart.

Ginger chased chastity. Becoming chaste involves two actions—turning from sexual sin and turning toward God. Indeed, in spiritual battle, to make a stand, you must move. ***Christians can take a stand against lust when they flee evil and pursue righteousness (2 Ti 2:22).*** *Through this pursuit, in your constant movement toward the prize, the world should see a difference between the way Christians and non-Christians live.*

Like Ginger, have you made a stand for chastity?
Give an example.

Bob Denver (Gilligan) felt that a sexy character like Ginger was unnecessary in a comedy show like *Gilligan's Island*.

Action / *Living On the Island...*

Lust—kill it before it kills you. Those who continue to feed their sinful desires risk incurring the wrath of God (Col 3:5-6). Like other sins, lust is an attempt to fill the loneliness in your life with worldly things. But a physical fix will never satisfy a spiritual hunger. Instead of lust, God wants you to fill your life with him in order to keep you from hurting yourself and others. Even if you are not troubled by sexually transmitted disease or unwanted pregnancy, lustful immorality can destroy your life by ruining honest, open relationships with your family and friends. Once saved, you must consider yourself dead to lust—because you are alive in Christ.

Why should you not lust?

How can you stop being lustful?

How can you become more chaste?

LUST...

COLOSSIANS 3:5-6
Put to death, therefore, whatever belongs to your earthly nature: sexual immorality, impurity, lust, evil desires... Because of these, the wrath of God is coming.

Judith Baldwin was the third actress to play Ginger—after Kit Smythe in the pilot episode and Tina Louise in the series.

THE STORY

This section, **"The Professor,"** puts the teacher to the test when he must choose between a) pride or b) humility at the University. After discovering that all of his new inventions have already been invented while he was away, the Professor dedicates himself to low-profile work on his obscure experiments. But the boastful Dean wants the famous Professor to focus on public speaking to promote the school. Now the Professor must learn a lesson on how to keep pride in—and out of—his work!

THE MORAL OF THE STORY

*This lesson, **"Pride in Your Work,"** highlights the Biblical principle of Pride. The study concentrates on how pride is sinful because it desires the self to be more important than others—even God. The notes also point out that humility is wise because it keeps a proper perspective, reducing self and elevating others. In summary, this lesson shows that, when we feel the prideful urge to compare, we should compare ourselves to Christ, who provides the example for our lives and loves us even when we fail.*

GILLIGAN'S ISLAND & THE SEVEN DEADLY SINS
Bible Study

lesson 4

SECTION TITLE: **"The Professor"**

LESSON TITLE: **"Pride in Your Work"**

BIBLICAL PRINCIPLE: **Pride**

PRIDE...

PROVERBS 16:18
Pride goes before destruction, a haughty spirit before a fall.

Galatians 6:4
Each one should test his own actions. Then he can take pride in himself, without comparing himself to somebody else,

"The Professor was the glue that held the more colorful characters in place in the *Gilligan* mosaic." Sherwood Schwartz

Parable / *A Three Hour Tour...*

For proud people to be so proud of themselves, they are not very self-aware. **In their celebration of self, they fail to acknowledge their weaknesses. Instead, they believe they are without faults and frailties. In their overconfidence, they set themselves up for a fall (Pr 16:18).** Indeed, pride brought about the fall of Lucifer from heaven to hell. This is why pride is considered the original and most serious sin—as well as a source of all other sins. Pride is sinful because it desires the self to be more important than others—even God. In a more subtle form, pride fails to give credit due to others while holding the self above its proper position.

Who showed pride—the Professor or the Dean?
Who showed humility? For each, how so?

Humility opposes pride. In fact, this virtue is often the lesson learned from pride. If pride is a blindfold that keeps us from seeing our faults, humility is a light that allows us to see ourselves as we truly are. ***When we look at ourselves with humility, we no longer feel the prideful desire to compare ourselves with others—but to be happy doing our best on our own (Gal 6:4).*** *Consider how the Professor changed.*

How did the Professor feel about his latest inventions?
How was he made humble?

Pride divides; humility heals both us and others. Pride, through competitive pressure, forces us apart. Humility, however, brings people together, with love and without judgment. ***When we feel the urge to boast, we should compare ourselves to Christ. His life provides the example for ours. And his love accepts us even when we fail. We should take pride in one thing—Christ died for us (Gal 6:14).*** *Think about the Professor's choice.*

Galatians 6:14
May I never boast except in the cross of our Lord Jesus Christ, through which the world has been crucified to me, and I to the world.

Why didn't the Professor promote himself?
Why did he choose his obscure work over public speaking?

Reflection / *Your Inner Gilligan...*

Pride leads to disgrace—which we foolishly bring upon ourselves (Pr 11:2). Whenever something good occurs in life, we should remember there is a fine line between thankful and prideful. Prideful people thank themselves for their good fortune. Wise people give credit to God. While the Lord wants you to be happy when good things happen, these are the times you must be most careful. It is one thing to feel on top of the world; it is quite another to look down on others from up there. This is how wisdom comes with humility. Humility is wise because it keeps a proper perspective, reducing self and elevating others, in accordance with the example of Christ. A humble person wisely acknowledges that the best things in life are really God-given blessings.

PRIDE...

PROVERBS 11:2
When pride comes, then comes disgrace, but with humility comes wisdom.

Like the Professor, have you had too much pride in your accomplishments? Give an example.

Russell Johnson was so good as the Professor that when video clips of his experiments were used to educate children, the students learned four times faster than from their regular teachers.

Matthew 23:12
"For whoever exalts himself will be humbled, and whoever humbles himself will be exalted."

The Professor got schooled in humility. It turned out he only thought he knew everything—and that is a big part of our problem with pride too. Oftentimes, to humble yourself, it takes the embarrassing realization that you are not as smart as you believed you were. In reality, nearly everyone will have that moment. ***When a person praises himself, God will humble him. But when a person is already humble, God will praise him (Mt 23:12).*** *Therefore, it is better to be humbler sooner rather than later.*

Like the Professor, has pride taught you a hard lesson in humility? Give an example.

James 1:9-10
The brother in humble circumstances ought to take pride in his high position. 10) But the one who is rich should take pride in his low position, because he will pass away like a wild flower.

The Professor shunned the spotlight for the Bunsen burner. While it is human nature to seek attention, unfortunately, pride will try to use any bit of approval to feed your ego. Those that make a deliberate choice to do good work in secret show they get their approval from a higher source. ***Those in low positions should be glad that worldly status means nothing to God. Similarly, those in high positions should also be glad status means nothing to God, because it so easily passes away (Jas 1:9-10).*** *What is in your heart—pride or humility—matters infinitely more.*

Like the Professor, have you shunned the spotlight for a more humble role? Give an example.

Bad Idea #3:
The studio executives said the Professor should actually be a bank robber on the lam who was only pretending to be a professor.

Action / *Living On the Island...*

God opposes the proud (Jas 4:6). Knowing this, if you continue to be proud, then you oppose God. In that, you put yourself in a very dangerous position. Fortunately, God allows you another option: if you are humble, you will receive his grace. Yet pride deceives you into thinking that you deserve everything you have and anything you want. It creates desires that actually corrupt your needs. The only way to be free of this hunger is by becoming humble before the Lord. Amazingly, seeking his approval will relieve the burden of your worldly desires. To avoid the punishments of pride, have the humility to ask God if self-satisfaction has blinded you.

Why should you not be prideful?

How can you stop being prideful?

How can you have more humility?

PRIDE...

JAMES 4:6
..."God opposes the proud but gives grace to the humble."

Unlike his character Gilligan, Bob Denver was actually known to be more like the Professor—extremely bright and very well read. In fact, he had been a teacher before becoming an actor.

THE STORY

This section, **"Thurston & Lovey Howell,"** shares the millionaire and his wife as they usually are—greedy & gluttonous—as well as how they should be—generous & restrained! At their dinner party, Thurston makes deals to make more money, and Lovey makes jaded jokes with jaded guests. But when Gilligan and the Skipper arrive, the Howells overhear their snobby guests insult their dear friends. And money and materialism go out the door—along with the guests—as the Howells gain the knowledge that their friends are the only thing they need more and more of!

THE MORAL OF THE STORY

*This lesson, "**More & More,**" highlights the Biblical principles of Greed and Gluttony. The notes focus on how both greed and gluttony are sinful because they seek their security in material things rather than God. The study also addresses that generosity opposes greed while restraint opposes gluttony. The goal of this lesson is that, for both greed and gluttony, generosity and restraint provide the right perspective on what we have: God has blessed us, so that we can bless others.*

GILLIGAN'S ISLAND & THE SEVEN DEADLY SINS

Bible Study

lesson 5

SECTION TITLE: **"Thurston & Lovey Howell"**

LESSON TITLE: **"More & More"**

BIBLICAL PRINCIPLES: **Greed & Gluttony**

GREED ...

LUKE 12:15
Then he said to them, "Watch out! Be on your guard against all kinds of greed; a man's life does not consist in the abundance of his possessions."

GLUTTONY...

PROVERBS 23:1-3
When you sit to dine with a ruler, note well what is before you, and put a knife to your throat if you are given to gluttony. Do not crave his delicacies, for that food is deceptive.

Titus 2:11-12
For the grace of God that brings salvation has appeared to all men. 12) It teaches us to say "No" to ungodliness and worldly passions, and to live self-controlled, upright and godly lives in this present age,

Parable / *A Three Hour Tour...*

Greed and gluttony are sins of excess—meaning both want more and more. **Greed focuses on acquiring wealth, usually at any cost, such as ignoring generosity. Ironically, the greedy man pursues temporary riches at the expense of eternal ones (Lk 12:15). Gluttony is often thought of as overindulgence of food and drink—but this sin also applies to materialism. In fact, the proverb cited warns against gluttony of money, not food: be careful when eating with an influential person because he may try to bribe you (Pr 23:1-3).** However, contrary to both greed and gluttony, Christ tells us that possessing a good life has little to do with our possessions. Rather than the latest possession that promises some sort of salvation, the truly good life comes from a relationship with God.

Who showed greed—Mr. Howell or his partners?
Who showed generosity? For each, how so?

Restraint goes against gluttony—it is the virtue that says "No" to the vice. A glutton not only consumes too much but refuses to share, thereby showing no sympathy for the needs of others. ***Restraint, on the other hand, can illustrate the grace of God as it teaches us to turn from ungodliness and live self-controlled lives because we are confident of our salvation in the Lord (Titus 2:11-12).*** *Consider how Mrs. Howell reacted to her dinner guests.*

Who showed gluttony—Mrs. Howell or her guests?
Who showed restraint? For each, how so?

Neither greed nor gluttony likes to lose. Indeed, these vices tell us to hoard as much as we can. ***However, if we practice generosity, the virtue that goes against greed, the Bible says we will get more by giving. This happens when we give and God provides more—so that the more we give, the more he provides for us to give. By contrast, the greedy and gluttonous person will come to ruin (Pr 11:24-25).*** *Think about how the Howells treated Gilligan and the Skipper.*

What did the Howells lose by siding with Gilligan and the Skipper? What did they gain?

Reflection / *Your Inner Gilligan...*

Greed and gluttony show insecurity. It isn't easy to look at—but it can motivate you to do better. **Both vices are sinful because they seek their security in material things rather than God (Lk 16:13).** When you are greedy or gluttonous, your actions say that God cannot take care of you. The truth is you simply are not satisfied with what he has provided you—namely, the opportunity to have a relationship with him. **Yet the only thing that will give you rest is the wisdom to trust God to meet your needs (Pr 23:4).** To receive this peace, first appreciate what you have instead of worrying about what you want. Secondly, strive to live with less instead of always wanting more. Thirdly, give from what you have rather than adding to your abundance. Through these steps, you may attain a better perspective on your possessions—and thank God for what he has provided you.

Like Mr. Howell, has seeing the greed of others spurred you to become more generous? Give an example.

Proverbs 11:24-25
One man gives freely, yet gains even more; another withholds unduly, but comes to poverty.
25) A generous man will prosper; he who refreshes others will himself be refreshed.

GREED...

LUKE 16:13
"No servant can serve two masters. Either he will hate the one and love the other, or he will be devoted to the one and despise the other. You cannot serve both God and Money."

GLUTTONY...

PROVERBS 23:4
Do not wear yourself out to get rich; have the wisdom to show restraint.

Because of her age, Natalie Schafer (Mrs. Howell) put in her contract that there would be no close-ups of her in the show.

Philippians 4:19
And my God will meet all your needs according to his glorious riches in Christ Jesus.

"No" wasn't always a word in Lovey's vocabulary. Similarly, some people simply refuse to have enough. A gluttonous person gives himself over to worldly passions—only to find that while he consumes them physically, they consume him spiritually. ***Conversely, restraint can bring freedom from obsession with our possessions, happiness from sharing with others and the approval of the Lord. God will meet all your needs—not necessarily your gluttonous wants (Ph 4:19).***

Like Mrs. Howell at first, have you refused to be satisfied? Give an example.

Psalm 112:5
Good will come to him who is generous and lends freely, who conducts his affairs with justice.

Thurston and Lovey refused to abuse their friends for money—a pretty big step for a Howell! Truly, your relationships with others are a thing too valuable to buy. Indeed, generosity of this sort shows three positive signs: it places people over money, it places others over self and it places faith in something higher than you to provide for you. ***In fact, for those who are generous and just, God promises a blessing (Ps 112:5).***

Like the Howells at the end, have you refused to benefit at the expense of others? Give an example.

Appropriately, when Jim Backus took the role of Mr. Howell, the money to be paid for the part had to be doubled.

Action / *Living On the Island...*

If you are greedy, turn from selfish gain (Ps 119:36-37). If you are gluttonous, resist your appetites (Jas 4:7). While no one is sufficient to do these things on their own, God will provide the security and strength you need to accomplish them. Tellingly, weak, insecure people usually lack the virtues of generosity and restraint. The fact that God loves you is already apparent from what he has previously given you—your life, family, friends, the opportunity to know him. Interestingly, when you begin to trust the Lord, your focus actually changes from your wants to others' needs, as you live less for self and more for him. For both greed and gluttony, generosity and restraint provide the right perspective on what you have: God has blessed you, so that you can bless others.

Why should you not be greedy?

How can you stop being gluttonous?

How will God provide for your needs?

GREED...

PSALM 119:36-37
Turn my heart toward your statutes and not toward selfish gain. Turn my eyes away from worthless things; preserve my life according to your word.

GLUTTONY...

JAMES 4:7
Submit yourselves, then, to God. Resist the devil, and he will flee from you.

Bad Idea #4: The studio executives said that the Howells should not be so rich because no one would identify with them.

THE STORY

This section, "**Mary Ann,**" gives the girl-next-door a fresh perspective on contentment as she goes from envious to envied on her wedding day—even though it may be the un-happiest day of her life! In her dressing room, Mary Ann cries because she and her old fiancé, who waited fifteen years, are now understandably unfamiliar. Luckily, Gilligan and the Skipper learn the maid of honor and the groom are really the ones in love! And Mary Ann sees why anyone who is green with envy is usually blue about it!

THE MORAL OF THE STORY

*This lesson, "**Green with Envy—and Blue About It,**" highlights the Biblical principle of Envy. The study examines how envy is sinful because, like other sins, it is an insatiable desire that puts the world before the Lord. The lesson also addresses how contentment comes when you ask God to give you the strength to overcome envious desires. The point of this study is that continuous contentment rests in your ability to maintain God's priorities, God's perspective and God as your source of fulfillment.*

GILLIGAN'S ISLAND & THE SEVEN DEADLY SINS

Bible Study

lesson 6

SECTION TITLE: **"Mary Ann"**

LESSON TITLE: **"Green with Envy—and Blue About It"**

BIBLICAL PRINCIPLE: **Envy**

ENVY...

PROVERBS 14:30
A heart at peace gives life to the body, but envy rots the bones.

Parable / *A Three Hour Tour...*

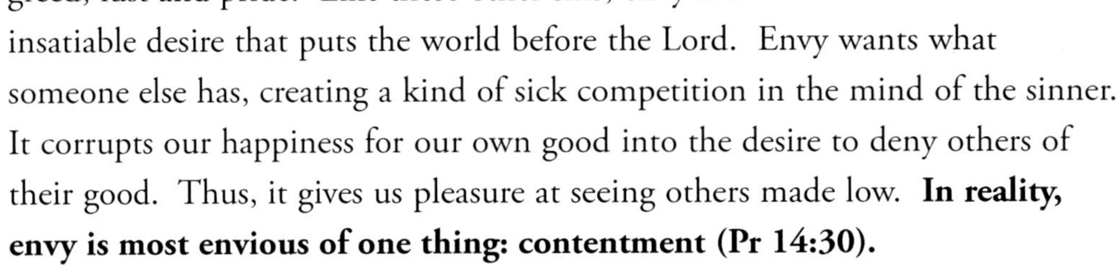

"So much to envy, so little time"—the mantra of the modern materialistic mind. Why is it that we always envy the lives of the rich and famous, yet we rarely envy the lives of the very holy? Sadly, too often what we envy is evil—the products of other sins such as greed, lust and pride. Like these other sins, envy is an insatiable desire that puts the world before the Lord. Envy wants what someone else has, creating a kind of sick competition in the mind of the sinner. It corrupts our happiness for our own good into the desire to deny others of their good. Thus, it gives us pleasure at seeing others made low. **In reality, envy is most envious of one thing: contentment (Pr 14:30).**

Who showed envy—Mary Ann or her friend Cindy?
Who showed contentment with the way things were? For each, how so?

James 3:14-15
But if you harbor bitter envy and selfish ambition in your hearts, do not boast about it or deny the truth.
15) Such "wisdom" does not come down from heaven but is earthly, unspiritual, of the devil.

If envy is the sickness, contentment is the cure. But how do we become content? ***The Bible indicates that a first step is to talk about our envy, not to boast but to reveal the truth. The truth here is that envy is foolishness—in fact, it is "wisdom" from the devil (Jas 3:14-15).*** *Envy inspires conflict, whereas Godly wisdom leads to peace. This is how the Lord delivers us from envy: he provides the contentment we seek. Consider how Cindy handled her envy.*

What should Cindy have done rather than suffer silently in envy?
How would talking to Mary Ann have brought contentment sooner?

Dawn Wells (Mary Ann) once competed for the 1960 Miss America title as Miss Nevada.

Envy is concerned with its own wants—not another's needs. This self-centeredness stunts the spiritual growth of envious people. In this state, they are easily controlled by their own desires, rather than having authority over those urges. Our goal should be to match our desires with God's desires. ***The Lord desires us to be peaceful, considerate, submissive and merciful (Jas 3:16-17).*** *Think about how Mary Ann conducted herself.*

Why was Mary Ann going through with the wedding?
How was she being considerate—to a fault?

James 3:16-17
For where you have envy and selfish ambition, there you find disorder and every evil practice. 17) But the wisdom that comes from heaven is first of all pure, then peace-loving, considerate, submissive, full of mercy and good fruit, impartial and sincere.

Reflection / *Your Inner Gilligan...*

Sinners envy sinners. The righteous fear the Lord (Pr 23:17). To envy evil is to literally sin over another's sin. This happens because the sin of envy leads you to idolize the sin of others. To break that cycle, you must idolize the ways of God. Those that seem to succeed while ignoring what God wants have a short-term gain—and a very-long-term loss. They cash in here for a miniscule amount of what they could have received in heaven. Even worse, what they ultimately get for their money or fame or status is eternal punishment. Lest you forget, there is a reason to fear the Lord. Seen in this light, sinners truly have nothing to envy.

Like Mary Ann, have you envied others?
Give an example.

ENVY...

PROVERBS 23:17
Do not let your heart envy sinners, but always be zealous for the fear of the Lord

Bad Idea #5:
The studio executives said Mary Ann should be completely cut out because the girl-next-door character had been done to death.

Galatians 5:26
Let us not become conceited, provoking and envying each other.

Mary Ann went from envious to envied—something she surely never expected! ***Yet despite how it may flatter you to be envied, you must discourage anyone from envying you (Gal 5:26).*** *You should re-direct any admiration of your accomplishments toward God. And at the same time, God must be the only one you look to for approval. When you do this, you will not need the approval of anyone else.*

Like Mary Ann, have you been surprised to find that others envy you? Give an example.

Philippians 4:11
...I have learned to be content whatever the circumstances.

Both Mary Ann and Cindy needed help to find contentment. ***The secret to lasting contentment, no matter your needs, is to draw on the power of Christ (Ph 4:11).*** *If you find yourself struggling with envy, ask God to strengthen you to overcome those desires. He will teach you contentment as you learn that he will take care of your needs—according to what he knows is best for you. Contentment comes when you rely on the Lord's promises.*

Like Cindy, has someone helped you to find contentment? Give an example.

The Castaway who got the most fan mail was Dawn Wells.

Action / *Living On the Island...*

You envy out of dissatisfaction and faithlessness. **This is one reason why God tells you to be content with what you have, and that he will never leave you (Heb 13:5).** Yet you envy because you feel empty. Your longing for possessions is really an attempt to fill a vacant place in your life. To fill this hole, rather than focusing on what you don't have, you should concentrate on what you could do for God. Make your priorities mirror his priorities. Then you will see life from the Lord's perspective. Continuous contentment rests in your ability to maintain God's priorities, God's perspective and God as your source of fulfillment.

Why should you not be envious?

How can you stop being envious?

How can you have contentment?

ENVY...

HEBREWS 13:5
...be content with what you have, because God has said, "Never will I leave you; never will I forsake you."

The characters of Mary Ann and Ginger were carefully contrasted in personalities and appearances—including heights and even hair colors.

THE STORY

This section, **"Here on Gilligan's Isle—Again,"** shows how the seven soon-to-be-re-stranded Castaways have learned to live together through the seven holy virtues. When the Professor laments they recently encountered the "Seven Deadly Sins" (his words!), Mary Ann remarks they never had those problems before—and the Skipper declares it is because they learned to get along. Then Gilligan fatefully suggests they all take another three hour tour. Fortunately, the Castaways continue to show signs of the seven holy virtues—even after they crash back on the island!

THE MORAL OF THE STORY

*This lesson, **"Seven Castaways, Seven Holy Virtues,"** highlights the Biblical principles of the Seven Holy Virtues. The notes look at how seven virtues were considered holy because they can redeem our relationships with God and man. The study also explains how all seven virtues—diligence, patience, chastity, humility, generosity, restraint and contentment—feature forgiveness, either of self or others. The core message here is that love covers all of the seven virtues, holding them together—which enables us to live together with others in unity and peace.*

GILLIGAN'S ISLAND & THE SEVEN DEADLY SINS
Bible Study

***lesson** 7*

SECTION TITLE: **"Here on Gilligan's Isle—Again"**

LESSON TITLE: **"Seven Castaways, Seven Holy Virtues"**

BIBLICAL PRINCIPLES: **Diligence, Patience, Chastity, Humility, Generosity, Restraint and Contentment**

7 HOLY VIRTUES...

COLOSSIANS 3:12
Therefore, as God's chosen people, holy and dearly loved, clothe yourselves with compassion, kindness, humility, gentleness and patience

Parable / *A Three Hour Tour...*

Whereas the seven deadly sins hurt us, the seven holy virtues can heal us. While the seven sins damage our love relationships with God and men, the seven virtues can redeem those relationships and thereby restore the life of grace that God wants us to live. **Like the seven sins, while the seven virtues are not listed by themselves in the Bible, their teaching was derived from scriptures like the one cited, in which 1) humility is represented by "humility," 2) patience is represented by "patience," 3) generosity is represented by "compassion," 4) restraint is represented by "kindness," 5) contentment (living at peace) is represented by "gentleness," 6) chastity is represented by "holy" and 7) diligence is represented by the application of each principle (Col 3:12).** The overall, shared objective of all these virtues is to live together with others in love.

Why didn't the Professor recall the Castaways dealt with the same seven deadly sins on the island that they encountered in civilization? Why didn't he immediately remember the sins of his friends?

Ephesians 4:2-3
Be completely humble and gentle; be patient, bearing with one another in love.
3) Make every effort to keep the unity of the Spirit through the bond of peace.

The virtues produce unity. ***While the selfishness of sin keeps us apart, the virtues—such as humility, gentleness and patience—create a bond that brings us together in peace (Eph 4:2-3).*** *This is so important because we are so imperfect. These virtues allow us to accept each other despite our faults—to see past what is wrong to what is right about another, and for that person to do the same for us. Consider what Mary Ann thought of life with the others.*

Why did Mary Ann explicitly state the Castaways *never* had a problem with the seven sins before? How did she view the time they lived together?

"The various characters learning to live together because they had to live together was the core of the series."
Sherwood Schwartz

The practice of these virtues takes just that—practice. Because it does not come naturally, the use of virtues may require a learning curve. ***The good news is we have a great teacher. The Holy Spirit at work in us produces fruit—or virtues—that are found in the character of Christ (Gal 5:22-23).*** *However, for this fruit to grow, we must continue to live for the Lord, using these virtues in our daily interactions with others. Think about why the Skipper thought they all got along.*

Galatians 5:22-23
But the fruit of the Spirit is love, joy, peace, patience, kindness, goodness, faithfulness, 23) gentleness and self-control. Against such things there is no law.

Was the Skipper right to say they learned to live together, despite their sins? On the island, how did they live out the seven holy virtues—diligence, patience, chastity, humility, generosity, restraint and contentment?

Reflection / *Your Inner Gilligan...*

All seven virtues feature forgiveness—either of self or others. Unfortunately, too often you forgive yourself but not any other. It is hard to live virtuously when all you do is disapprove of people. The main thing to remember about forgiving others is how much God has forgiven you. Ask yourself: is whatever you need to forgive in someone else any worse than what the Lord has already forgiven in you? **Understanding how much God loves and forgives you will enable you to do the same with others (Col 3:13).** Then you will be free to live virtuously.

7 HOLY VIRTUES...

COLOSSIANS 3:13
Bear with each other and forgive whatever grievances you may have against one another. Forgive as the Lord forgave you.

Like the Castaways, have you forgiven yourself while accusing others of sin? Give an example.

"Situation comedy series once helped bring the family unit closer together, with the kind of positive social reality that predominated in the households in this country."
Sherwood Schwartz

Romans 12:18
If it is possible, as far as it depends on you, live at peace with everyone.

The Castaways lived in peace—seemingly despite themselves. When you accept someone as his sinful self, you are not excusing his sins but embracing the sinner. To comfort the person is not necessarily to condone his misdeeds. ***Rather it is a way of saying that the person is better than the sin. This peaceful ideal is at the core of Christian living (Ro 12:18).*** *It is based on God's grace—which once you have experienced, you will want others to experience through you.*

Like the Castaways, have you lived in peace with friends, despite their imperfections? Give an example.

1 Corinthians 13:4-5
Love is patient, love is kind. It does not envy, it does not boast, it is not proud. 5) It is not rude, it is not self-seeking, it is not easily angered, it keeps no record of wrongs.

The Castaways made fast friends—and faster enemies. While it is easy to treat friends with love, it is even easier to not *treat enemies this way.* ***But the Bible tells us that love prominently includes the virtues of patience and kindness—and explicitly excludes the sins of envy, pride, selfishness (which also covers greed and gluttony) and anger, while obviously opposing lust as well (1 Cor 13:4-5).*** *God wants you to love everyone equally—and only through him can you do it.*

Unlike the Castaways, have you treated both friends and enemies equally with love? Give an example.

"It was in half-hour comedies that stories featured the value of people's relationships, the importance of truth, love, learning, integrity, etc."
Sherwood Schwartz

Action / *Living On the Island...*

Love covers all of the seven virtues, holding them together—which enables us to live together with others in unity and peace (Col 3:14). Notably, none of the seven sins feature love. And any attempt to practice the seven virtues without love is doomed to fail. To live out the seven virtues: study God's Word, act like Jesus and experience his love in your heart. Remember, Christ lived without the seven sins, practiced the seven virtues (and more!) and gave his life out of love for you.

Why should you shun the seven deadly sins?

How can you practice the seven holy virtues?

How can you communicate God's love, forgiveness and grace to others?

7 HOLY VIRTUES...

COLOSSIANS 3:14
And over all these virtues put on love, which binds them all together in perfect unity.

"Gilligan's Island, along with other situation comedies, always stressed these nobler attributes in the human condition."
Sherwood Schwartz

DEDICATION:

Father

Son

Holy Spirit